UNTITLED SUBJECTS

BOOKS BY

RICHARD HOWARD

POETRY

Untitled Subjects   *1969*
The Damages   *1967*
Quantities   *1962*

CRITICAL

Alone with America   *1969*

UNTITLED SUBJECTS

POEMS BY

RICHARD HOWARD

New York ATHENEUM *1969*

"1851" appeared, under the title "John Ruskin: A Message from Denmark Hill," in NEW AMERICAN REVIEW.

"1852" appeared, under the title "Pastoral Remains," in the QUARTERLY REVIEW OF LITERATURE.

"1864" appeared, under the title "The Other Author," in PARTISAN REVIEW.

"1891" appeared, under the title "Freshwater: An Idyll," in POETRY.

"1915" appeared, under the title "A Pre-Raphaelite Ending," in NEW AMERICAN REVIEW.

Library of Congress catalog card number 78–86548
Published simultaneously in Canada by McClelland and Stewart Ltd
Manufactured by Kingsport Press, Inc.,
Kingsport, Tennessee
Designed by Harry Ford
First Printing September 1969
Second Printing September 1970

To my friend **RENAUD BRUCE,** *who has taught me the rewards of an interest in other people, I dedicate these poems, less presumptuously than if I were to inscribe them, as well, to the great poet of otherness whose initials are the same and who said, as I should like to say, "I'll tell my state as though 'twere none of mine."*

CONTENTS

NOTES

1801   *The speaker had settled in England in 1771 on Garrick's invitation to superintend scene painting at Drury Lane. The Envoy to Constantinople was the seventh Earl of Elgin, who arranged for the Parthenon frieze to be conveyed to England in 1803.*

1825   *The speaker is Sir Walter Scott, whose observations extend over several years.*

1851   *The speaker is John Ruskin, on his wedding journey in Venice.*

1852   *The speaker is the vicar of Boulge, whose imaginary but characteristic diaries constitute his entire literary remains.*

1821–1824–1857   Il Signor Crescendo *was one nickname of Gioachino Rossini.*

1858   *Leaves from the diary of a Member's wife, a lady of fashion.*

1864   *The speaker is probably Thackeray, who called himself "the other novelist"—i.e., not Dickens—though there is no record of Thackeray's having had a son.*

1876   *The speaker is Lady Trevelyan, whose son George had undertaken to write a biography of her brother, the late Lord Macaulay.*

1882   *Sir Moses Montefiore furthered the political emancipation of Jews in Europe and the growth of the Zionist movement.*

1889   *Alassio is a seaside resort southwest of Genoa, long favored by English expatriates.*

1824–1889   *An apostrophe to Wilkie Collins, born 1824, died 1889.*

1891   Freshwater *was Tennyson's estate on the Isle of Wight.*

1897   *The speaker is Gladstone's secretary, though not so celebrated a one as John Morley, who by this date was already a Member of Parliament.*

1907   *The recipient of this proposal may well have been Arnold Schoenberg, though of course the latter's tone poem on the subject proposed was composed in 1905.*

1915   *The speaker is Mrs. William Morris, addressing her daughter May, a spinster in her late forties.*

UNTITLED SUBJECTS

1801

Among the Papers of the Envoy to Constantinople

May it please Lord Elgin, Earl of Kincardine,
to consider the undersign'd, sole author
and inventor of the Eidophusikon,

for the position so lately rejected
by Mr. Turner. On giving the measure
of its Effects, calm & storm both, sunset

or moonlight, the accurate imitation
of Nature's sounds: approaching thunder, the dash
of waves on a pebbly beach, the distant gun—

my Device was pronounc'd by no less a judge
than Richard Wilson, R.A.—the same who cried out
at the sight of Terni Cascade, "O well done,

water, by God!"—was pronounc'd, I say, by him
"highly successful in agitated seas,"
by reason of the high finish carrying

severally their satellites of colour
into the very center of the Pictures.
As it happens, your Lordship, I visited

the same Joseph Turner known to your Lordship
(I believe) only this week, and found a man
pacing to and fro before his pale muslin

on which the sick and wan Sun, in all the doubt
of darkness, was not allow'd to shed one ray,
but tears. Even as he work'd, pouring wet paint

onto paper till it was saturated,
then tore, then scratch'd, then scrubb'd in a frenzy
at the sheet, the Whole being chaos, until

as if by enchantment, the Scene appear'd then,
great ships gone to pieces in order to fling
magical oranges on the waves—but I

digress: even as he shew'd me two books fill'd
with studies from Nature, several tinted
on the spot—which he found, he said, much the most

valuable to him—this Turner discuss'd
the present urgency of your Lordship's need
for an artist who might draw Antiquities,

with suitable finish, before Removal,
by your Lordship's design, from Athens. He said
he could not, himself, endure the Ideal,

but enjoy'd and look'd for only *litter*—why
even his richest vegetation is confus'd,
he delights in shingle, debris, and mere heaps

of fallen stone. Upon communicating
the intelligence that your Lordship's stipend
must include assistance to Lady Elgin

in decorating fire-screens and the like,
the man turn'd back in some heat to his labour
upon what I took to be that mysterious

forest below London Bridge, where great ships ride,
sails filling or falling, disorder'd too
by the stress of anchorage, all beautiful

though wild beneath the Daemonic pressure
of his inquiry (with so much of the trowel,
surely a touch more *finishing* might be borne!).

Enough of Turner, I have not to speak here
of him, though what I saw was but the *scribbling*
of Painting, surely. What I would say is this:

I venture to suggest in myself a man
your Lordship, and my Lady, most certainly,
might rely upon for accurate Service,

work of a conclusive polish, not a sketch.
There is, may I make so bold, a point at which
in Turner's Picturesque, as Fuseli says,

two spiders, caressing or killing each other,
must have greatly the advantage, in roughness
of surface and intricacy of motion,

over every athletic or am'rous
Symplegma left by the Ancients. I do not
wish to speak further of the man who renounc'd

your Lordship's commission to copy marbles,
muttering (though plain to hear) "Antiquities
be damn'd, by Thames' shore we will die," and went on

raking at the sea with his untidy thumb;
but only to call your Lordship's kind notice
and gracious favour, for the appointed task,

to the creator of the Eidophusikon,
these many years a loyal British subject,
Yours, &c.

PHILIPPE-JACQUES DE LOUTHERBOURG.

1825

But high & perilous enterprise is not the man's forte. He would never have been his celebrated ancestor Sir Nigel, but only Sir Nigel's eulogist & poet. I shall tell you where he is at home, my dear, & in his place—in the lettered indolence & elegant enjoyments of Waverly-Honour. And he will refit the old library in the most exquisite Gothic taste, & garnish its shelves with the rarest volumes, & he will draw plans & landscapes & write verses & rear temples & dig grottoes, & he will stand on a clear summer night in the colonnade before the Hall & gaze on the deer as they stray in the moonlight or lie in shadow beneath the boughs of the huge old fantastic oaks, & he will repeat the verses to his wife who will hang upon his arm; & he will be a happy man. WAVERLY

I have all my life regretted I did not keep
    A journal, regular to the day;
    That such custom of a diary
Might make me wiser or better I dare not say,
       And must not over-puff
My little collection of curiosities—
    With all his talents, Horace Walpole
    Makes a silly figure when he gives
Upholsterer's catalogues of Strawberry Hill—

Yet now we have published the W. Novels
    (Popular Edition) which will end
    After forty-eight volumes the set,
And shall begin the Poetical Works in twelve
      With vignettes by Turner,
Is it not the time? If once you turn on your side,
    Sir Walter, after the hour you ought
    To rise, it is all over. Bolt up
At once: lime rubbish dug in among the roots

Of ivy encourages it much—to keeping
    Journals then! Wrote six of these pages
    Close yesterday; what is more, I think
It comes off twangingly. Gad, my bile is quite gone,
    A wondrous connexion
Between the mind and body! An odd thought strikes me:
    When I die will this book of my days
    Be taken from the tall ebony
Cabinet and read as but the transient pout

Of a man worth one hundred sixty thousand pounds,
    With wonder the well-seeming Bart.
    Should ever have suffered such a hitch?
Or will it be found in some obscure lodging-house
    Wherein the decayed son
Of chivalry has hung up his scutcheon for some
    Twenty shillings a week, and old friends
    Look grave and whisper, "Pity he took
That foolish title"—who can answer this question?

Bad night, last. Bad dreams about poor Charlotte. Awoke,
    Thinking my old and inseparable
    Friend beside me; only when I got
Fully awake could I persuade myself that she
    Was dark, low and distant,
And that my bed was widowed. Our match was something
    Short of love in all its forms, but love
    I suspect comes only once a life:
People nearly drowned don't venture a second time

Out of their depths. God help us! Earth, I know, cannot.
    A boding sense, this morning, that all
    My exertions may prove useless, yet

To save Abbotsford I would attempt anything:
    My heart clings to the place
I have created, scarce a tree on it but owes
      Its being to me, and forfeiture
      Looms a greater pain than I can tell:
The public favour is my only lottery.

Yet there might be economies: I am not bound
      To stand Mine Host to all of Scotland
      And England as I do; the Great Hall
Begins to be haunted by too much company
      Of every carl and kind,
Especially foreigners. I do not like them.
      I hate fine waistcoats & pearl breast-pins
      Upon dirty shirts; I detest talk
Of nothing more than having seen—last year, I vow!—

The Lady of the Lake at the Opera . . . Nor
      Does a young Lord who lies on the rug
      And looks poetical take my heart,
Even in Dutch! Last week, some Italian signors
      Landed here, but as we—
Neither party—dared speak bad French, I must give them
      A good breakfast in silence: civil
      Gentlemen trying to be understood,
And I not knowing which was the interpreter.

After all, it is not my fault: who would see me
      Should be able to speak my language,
      Not sit, never knowing what to make
Of himself in the forenoon, tormenting the ladies . . .
      I love the round virtues
Of a rough man; others escape into salt-rheum,
      Sal-volatile and a white pocket-

Handkerchief. Take little Moore, *there* is
Good breeding for you: not the least touch of the poet!

I saw him this recentest journey to London,
        Delighted ever by his manly
        Frankness. We visited Kenilworth
Together. Unrelenting rain allowed only
        A glimpse of the ruin:
Yet the last time I was there these trophies of Time
        Were quite neglected. Now they approach
        So much nearer to splendour as to have
A door at least if not windows. They are, in short,

Preserved and protected. That much for the Novels.
        Walked from one till half-past four (morning
        Was damp, dripping and unpleasant). Dogs
Took a hare: they most always catch one on Sunday,
        A Puritan would say
The Devil was in them. A visit after this,
        Proving my stricture on Foreigners
        Extravagant—but a Frenchman is
Either the best or the worst company one has—

For tea, varied with camomile, from
        Audubon the ornithologist
        And a boy, sixteen, name of Darwin
Studying from him how to stuff such birds & beasts
        As are found in Scotland,
Though he passes for a medical student here.
        Audubon teaches him the science
        Without expense, owning a Negro
To accomplish all the *disagreeable parts,*

As he calls the gutting. The lad seems dull enough,
        No match at the tea for Audubon

Who has followed that pursuit of his
By many a long wandering in the dark woods
        Of North America.
No dash or glimmer about him: he wears long hair
    Time has not yet tinged, his countenance
    Handsome and acute. Spoke with him
Much of beasts (the drawings are of the first order).

Another day of wet. Enter Rheumatism
    And takes me by the knee. Yet I am
    Of opinion pain is an evil!
Remembering how I once murdered McLellan
        At Thrieve Castle and stabbed
The Black Douglas in Stirling, astonished King James
    Before Roxborough and stifled the Earl
    Of Mar in his bath at Canongate,
It is a tame pasture you limp through now, Sir—

A wild world, my masters, this braw Scotland of ours
    Must have been! With Audubon again
    Looked into a show of wild beasts here,
And saw Nero the great lion, noble creature,
        Like a Prince at *levée*
In a large cage where you might be let in with him:
    I had a month's mind, but was afraid
    Of the newspapers; of nothing else,
For never did creature seem more gentle and yet

Majestic—I longed to caress him. Audubon
    Says the whole frame (mine and Nero's too)
    Is in all its parts and divisions
Gradually in the act of decaying and
        Renewing. A curious
Timepiece that could tell when this insensible change

11

Had been so wrought in a man that no
Atom was left of the original
Who had existed at a certain season, but

Boasted in his stead another having the same
Limbs, thews and sinews, lineaments
The same—a pair of transmigrated
Stockings like Sir John Cutler's, all green silk without
One thread of the first black
Remaining. Odd to be at once another and
The same. Am I then the child crying
To protest his mother's decision—
I see her still, dressed to go out of an evening,

And I hear the sentence, admitting no appeal:
"No, no, Watty canna understand
The great Mr. Garrick, mauna go."
I am indignant *yet* at the supposition—
So I am that Watty
Somewhere, even now, if I cannot name the place.
In truth, such fancies divert us, though
I do not compare myself in point
Of fancy's highest flight with Wordsworth, far

From that. Yet I can see as many blue castles
In the clouds as any honest man,
As many genii in the curling
Smoke of a steam-engine, as perfect
A Persepolis grown
In the embers of a sea-coal fire. All my life
Has been spent in such day-dreams, but I
Cry no roast-meat for that . . . Still deep snow,
A foot thick in the courtyard, I dare say: severe

Welcome to the new lambs coming into the world.
    But what signifies, whether they die
    Just now or a little while after,
To be united with salad at luncheon? It
      Signifies a good deal:
There is a period, though a short one, when they dance
    Among the gowans and seem happy
    Though the rigs bear nothing more to rouse
The heart but windle-straes and sandy lavrocks. Just so.

Accounting for such things, I become enamored
    Of my Journal. May the zeal but last . . .

1851

My dearest father, it is the year's First Day,
    Yet so like the Last, in Venice, no one
        Could tell this birth from the lees.
           I know it is some while
Since you received a word of mine: there has been
    The shabbiest sort of interruption
        To our exchanges (to mine
           At least) in the shape
Of a fever—nights of those imaginings,
    Strange but shameful too, of the Infinite
        By way of bedcovers and
           Boa constrictors,
With cold wedges of ice, as I thought, laid down
    At the corners of the bed, making me
        Slip to its coiling center
           Where I could not breathe.
You knew from my last, I think, I had again
    Gone to the Zoological Gardens
        And seen the great boa take
           Rabbits, which gave me
An idea or two, and a headache. Then
    I had too much wine that same night, & dreamed
        Of a walk with Nurse, to whom
           I showed a lovely
Snake I promised her was an innocent one:
    It had a slender neck with a green ring
        Round it, and I made her feel
           The scales. When she bade
Me feel them too, it turned to a fat thing, like

A leech, and adhered to my hand, so that
I could scarcely pull it off—
And I awakened
(So much, father, for my serpentine fancies)
To a vermillion dawn, fever fallen,
And the sea horizon dark,
Sharp & blue, and far
Beyond it, faint with trebled distance, came on
The red vertical cliffs in a tremor
Of light I could not see without
Recalling Turner
Who had taught me so to see it, yet the whole
Subdued to one soft gray. And that morning
I had your letter, father,
Telling of the death
Of my earthly master. How much more I feel
This now (perhaps it is worth noting here
The appearance of my first
Gray hair, this morning)
—More than I thought I should: everything
In the sun, in the sky so speaks of him,
So mourns their Great Witness lost.
Today, the weather
Is wretched, cold and rainy, dark like England
At this season. I do begin to lose
All faith in these provinces.
Even the people
Look to me ugly, except children from eight
To fourteen, who here as in Italy
Anywhere are glorious:
So playful and bright
In expression, so beautiful in feature,
So dark in eye and soft in hair—creatures

Quite unrivalled. At fifteen
They degenerate
Into malignant vagabonds, or sensual
Lumps of lounging fat. And this latter-day
Venice, father! where by night
The black gondolas
Are just traceable beside one, as if Cadmus
Had sown the wrong teeth and grown dragons, not
Men. The Grand Canal, this month,
Is all hung, from end
To end, with carpets and tapestries like a street
Of old-clothes warehouses. And now there is
Even talk of taking down,
Soon, Tintoretto's
Paradise to "restore" it. Father, without
The Turner Gallery, I do believe
I should go today and live
In a cave on some
Cliffside—among crows. O what fools they are, this
Restoring pack, yet smoothing all manner
Of rottenness up with words.
My Turner would not
Phrase like these, and only once in all the years
I knew him said, "Thank you, Mr. Ruskin."
My own power, if it be that,
Would be lost by mere
Fine Writing. You know I promised no Romance—
I promised them Stones. Not even bread.
Father, I do not feel any
Romance in Venice!
Here is no "abiding city", here is but
A heap of ruins trodden underfoot
By such men as Ezekiel
Angrily describes,

Here are lonely and stagnant canals, bordered
    For the most part by blank walls of gardens
        (Now waste ground) or by patches
            Of mud, with decayed
Black gondolas lying keel-upmost, sinking
    Gradually into the putrid soil.
        To give Turner's joy of this
            Place would not take ten
Days of study, father, or of residence:
    It is more than joy that must be the great
        Fact I would teach. I am not sure,
            Even, that joy is
A fact. I am certain only of the strong
    Instinct in me (I cannot reason this)
        To draw, delimit the things
            I love—oh not for
Reputation or the good of others or
    My own advantage, but a sort of need,
        Like that for water and food.
            I should like to draw
All Saint Mark's, stone by stone, and all this city,
    Oppressive and choked with slime as it is
        (Effie of course declares, each
            Day, that we must leave:
A woman cannot help having no heart, but
    That is hardly a reason she should have
        No manners), yes, to eat it
            All into my mind—
Touch by touch. I have been reading *Paradise*
    Regained lately, father. It seems to me
        A parallel to Turner's
            Last pictures—the mind
Failing altogether, yet with intervals
    And such returns of power! "Thereupon

Satan, bowing low his gray
Dissimulation,
Disappeared." Now he is gone, *my* dark angel,
And I never had such a conception
Of the way I must mourn—not
What I lose, now, but
What I *have* lost, until now. Yet there is more
Pain knowing that I must forget it all,
That in a year I shall have
No more *awareness*
Of his loss than of that fair landscape I saw,
Waking, the morning your letter arrived,
No more left about me than
A fading pigment.
All the present glory, like the present pain
Is no use to me; it hurts me rather
From my fear of leaving it,
Of losing it, yet
I know that were I to stay here, it would soon
Cease being glory to me—that it *has*
Ceased, already, to produce
The impression and
The delight. I can bear only the first days
At a place, when all the dread of losing
Is lost in the delirium
Of its possession.
I daresay love is very well when it does not
Mean *leaving behind,* as it does always,
Somehow, with me. I have not
The heart for more now,
Father, though I thank you and mother for all
The comfort of your words. They bring me,
With *his* loss, to what I said
Once, the lines on this

Place you will know: "The shore lies naked under
  The night, pathless, comfortless and infirm
    In dark languor, still except
      Where salt runlets plash
Into tideless pools, or seabirds flit from their
  Margins with a questioning cry." The light
    Is gone from the waters with
      My fallen angel,
Gone now as all must go. Your loving son,

                        J O H N .

1852

Last night I looked out before
Going up to bed:
The air seemed perfectly still,
Frosty, and the stars ablaze. I could hear
Some continuous moaning
Sound I knew to be
Not that of a child exposed
Or female ravished, but of the Sea,
More than ten miles off! Little
Wind up as there was,
It carried me the murmurs
Of the waves ever circulating round
These coasts and so far over
A flattened country . . .
Read late—the *Suasoriae*,
And I wonder whether old Seneca
Was indeed such a humbug
As people now say:
He shows how philosophy
Stood when the gods had worn out a good deal.
I don't think the man believed
He should live again:
Death was his great resource . . . I shall go
To London soon, visiting
Carlyle once the Spring
Is farther out. Completed
His *Latter-Day Pamphlets*, too much cut up
Into short squibs: one labours
Through it as ships do
In what is called a short sea—

Small contrary waves caused by shallows,
    Straits and meeting tides. I like
        To sail 'fore the wind
    Over a long eloquence,
Like the Opium-Eater's. There is
    Good fresh-water faring, too,
        In some Addison.
    Is there any *pond*-sailing
To speak of in literature? I mean,
    Drowsy, slow, of small compass?
        Perhaps in my sermons . . .
    The cold wears on, I pity
Those poor mistaken lilac-buds there
    Out the window, and one old
        Robin, ruffled up
    To his thickest, mournfully
Sitting under them, quite disheartened . . .
    Here is a glorious day
        Which I welcomed in
    At the spinet with Handel's
Coronation Anthems, where human Pomp
    Is to be accompanied
        And illustrated.
    Sunshine all the morning since,
While I read about Nero in Tacitus,
    Lying full length on a bench
        In the garden-close:
    A nightingale singing, and
Not far away some red anemones
    Manfully eyeing the sun.
        Curious mixture
    All this: Nero and the Spring's
Delicacy—very human though. Very.
    Coming in, I settle down

To accounts, my sister
Winding gray wool from the back
Of a chair, her baby girl chattering:
So runs the world away. You
Might suppose I live
In Epicurean ease, but
This is a good day: one is not always
Well, the weather always clear,
Nightingales singing,
Nor Tacitus full of such
Pleasant atrocity. But such as life is,
I believe I have got hold
Of a goodish end . . .
Journeys, even to London,
Are a vanity. The *soul* remains the same.
Now the black trees opposite
In the Regent's Park
Begin showing green buds, and men
Come by with great baskets of flowers:
Primroses, hepaticas,
Crocuses and huge
Daisies, calling as they go,
"Growing, growing! All the glory going!"
Some old street cry, it would make
You smell them almost
From Calcutta. All the glory
Going! Yesterday smoked a pipe with Carlyle
We ascended from his parlor,
Carrying our pipes
Up through two storeys, and got
Into a little room near the roof: there
We sat, the window open,
And looked out—or down—
On gardens, their almond trees

In blossom and beyond, bare walls, and over
    These, roofs and chimneys, often
      A steeple, and the whole
Of London crowned with darkness
Gathering behind like the fathomless pool
    Of some dream: it melts away
      All life into one
    Common lump . . . Here, John, I am
Home, run with the Crucifix and the Missal
    To the Hermitage, and set
      The fountain going . . .
    A week of writing. I take
What Liberties I like, but am not
    Poet enough to be frightened
      From such excursions:
    And withal, I think, really
I have the faculty of making something
    Readable. Yet I only
      Sketch out the matter,
    Then put it off. When I die
What a farrago of these will be found! . . .
    Today, through green fields, we made
      A pick-nick, only
    Up the Thames, for I am not
Heroick enough for Castles, Battlefields
    And such things. Strawberry Hill
      Must do, and has done.
    I looked all over it, though
Pictures, jewels, curiosities were sold
    Ten years ago: only bare
      Stones remain, haply
    Stuck with the Gothick woodwork
And ceilings sometimes painted Gothick
    To imitate such woodwork:

All a Toy, but yet
The Toy of a clever man.
The rain comes through the roofs, and is slowly
Loosening the cornices'
Confectionary
Battlements. Who reads Walpole
Now? That world is gone. I remember—
How well!—when we used to be
In the nursery,
And from the window watch hounds
Course over the lawn, Father and Mr. Jem
In their hunting caps and long
Whips, I can see them!
All Daguerrotyped into
The mind's eye now, fancy being civilized
Enough to know what a thing
Daguerrotype is!
No more I do, nor need to:
Among the scenes in that novel called The Past,
These dwell most in memory.
What is the difference
Between what has been and what
Has never been? None, or none that I can tell.

1821-1824-1857

Scenes from the life of Il Signor Crescendo

for Michael DiCapua

I: *1821*

Rome, and in Carnival, allows
Only a momentary glimpse before
    Another fit of revelry
Intercepts our view. Quick, look at that patch
    Of red wall at the corner—no,
Farther to the left: there. Now watch closely,
    You will see them appear, playing
Guitars (furiously), singing their lungs out.

The tall one in a black apron
Has a huge hooked nose you will recognize
    Despite his street-singer's costume;
And all the black lace in the world (which he
    Has on, I think) cannot disguise
A jaw like a blue lantern shining through
    Layers of powder. An aura
Of the Satanic lingers in the way

He moves his hands (only last night
They performed—"Divine!" "Diabolical!"—
    At the Principessa d'Este's,
Two dozen Transcendental Caprices
    And a Cavatinetta for
The Violin Upside Down, which blur now
    In a din of diamonds
Across the strings of the festooned guitar).

But it is the other Mask
We are concerned with: *piccolo* beside
        His contra-bassoon of a friend
(Who made him cry the first time in his life,
        He claims, by those same Caprices),
And at thirty so stout that he must strum
        His obbligato off one hip;
He has written thirty-one operas—

        Next year he will meet Beethoven,
Catch syphilis and become a European
        Institution, but now he is
Just adorable in pink (the mantilla
        Colbran wore in *The Barber*)
And no more than an Italian lover
        Of Mozart ("I can set laundry
Lists"—what else was "*Il Catalogo?*").

They form, before that crumbling red plaster,
        A period composition—
The pink, the black, the bright ribbons floating
        Like the tune—some minor master
Of the genre might have painted it, down
        To the last sequin and the first
Suggestion, round the fat feminine lips,
        Of a certain bitterness: fun
Is fun, *basta*! Folly a kind of fate.

    II: *1824*

        Carlton House: the Saloon.
    The favorite horses of the First
Gentleman of Europe course around the panels

In George Stubbs' famous frescoes while
The Royal George, beneath them, falls
A victim, like so many common cavaliers,
     To the relentless spell:
     It is the "Willow Song"
Another fat friend offers, Desdemona's
     "*Salce*" falsetto, recalling
     In each clear roulade the heartless
Adepts of the old Italian school, banished
     Now these many years from the stage
          For the offence they caused
          British modesty and
     British manliness. Lord Byron
Himself (who like most of those sweet singers is dead
          —The news but not yet the body
     Lately brought from the swamps of Greece)
Deplored the sorry contrast between the bloated
          Trunks of men and a girl's
          Tessitura, adding
"These half-fellows should not be seen." And yet the King,
     No whit deterred by any such
     Affront, actual or fancied,
To his . . . *proprieties,* proposes a duet:
     "I ever affected artists
          Such as yourself, Signor.
          The first of our poets,
     Sir Walter Scott, ye know, was turned
Baronet by this hand." "Yes, Sire," comes the answer
     From the spinet, "and by this one
     Or these, *The Lady of the Lake*
An opera." Prince Leopold of Saxe-Coburg
     (In six years to be elected
          King of all the Belgians
          By the help of God's hand

And the logic of Succession)

And the Duchess of Kent (whose daughter Victoria

Is too young for so late an event)

Are among the great company

Whose grief for the Greeks' lost saviour is a little

Assuaged by the Maestro's *Pianto*

Delle Muse in Morte

Di Lord Byron. After

Which he confides to all

That except for Paganini's playing, the sole

Occasion that drew from him tears

Was the *fiasco* of his first

Opera. And when (just under the *White Stallion*

Frightened by a Lion,

"Prinny"—King George IV—

In a bass as flabby as his figure commences

The great *scena buffa* between

Dandini and Don Magnifico

From *Cenerentola*, suddenly breaking off

To beg pardon (the King to beg!)

For a mistake in time—

(You see them now, don't you?

By the sconces on the spinet

That pick out the gilt moldings, the gaunt thoroughbreds

Galloping overhead,

The two obesities

At graces or at grips —"Which of all your operas,

Signor, do you the most affect?"

"*Don Giovanni*, Sire"—

The Royal one in military dress, a great

Pair of spurs half-way up his leg

Like a gamecock, Rossini

In rose, alas, and green:

You see? You hear?)—when George falters,

Rossini, with a bow that produces a faint chord
      Where his corpulence strikes
      The keys, replies at once,
"Sire, you have every right to do just as you please;
      I shall follow Your Majesty
      To the grave." Which is also true.

III: *1857*

      To all appearance,
A furnished house in the Rue de la Pompe,
      Passy. We are in what the French
      Have always called, with unlikely
Frankness, a Winter Garden—the chilly
      Little room contains
A pair of perfectly immense persons,
      Six chipped pots of squamous cacti
      And, crawling over the glazed bricks
Glassed in with the black Pleyel & two chairs,
      A posthumous vine.
Leaf by shrivelling leaf the ivy scrawls
      Its message to the occupants:
      The writing on the wall will be
No longer in a fine Italian hand.
      Envious Weber,
Meyerbeer the Jew Banker, and Wagner
      Who has "some beautiful moments
      But more bad quarters of an hour"—
Have taken opera out of his hands
      These twenty-nine years.
Rossini's hands! Which as he sits to play
      In slippers and a slipping wig
      He can no longer clasp across

That listless corporation of his, so
  Touches only treble
Or bass keys—*La Musique Anodine*,
  He calls it when he sings to her
  (To Olympe, the motherly whore
He's long since made an honest helpmate of);
  Sings for the first time
Since *Tell*, and for the first time ever to
  His own words; and now the only
  Diamonds Olympe wears are on
Her cheeks. "Tears, *carina?* Have I told you,
  The only three times
I ever cried were when *La Cambiale* failed,
  When first I heard Niccolo play,
  And once, in a gondola, when
A turkey stuffed with truffles fell over-
  Board." Olympe smiles, and
To sustain the joke, as he always could,
  The fat sick man in the *jardin*
  D'hiver plays his wife his latest:
La Chanson du Bébé it's called, "baby"
  Being the giant
Infant thumping, tinkling through this last gift
  Before a still longer silence
  Falls than the last because it is
The last. How right, then, and how . . . Rossini,
  That of all his gifts
This final song to celebrate a good
  Stool, this toilet-training aria
  Should praise (he died of a rectal
Fistula) that first gift—*Maman, pipi!*
  Papa, cacaaa!
—ever made, made over in one last song.

1858

JUNE

. . . To the beach with Bella, and beyond
   the wicked Pavillion, went
into that bathing-machine, where I
   undressed and entered the sea,
(the first time in my life!) a woman
   attending me all the while;
I thought it delightful, till I put
   my head under the water,
when I feared lest I should be stifled.
   Ladies about, with such hair—
long, damp, hanging down to dry, and not
   so much as a handkerchief
to cover it—just like so many
   penitents, I could not help
thinking, yet dear Bella only barked
   the more when a wave ran high,
and all those tresses drowned once again . . .

JULY

. . . The Londonderry Packet. (Old Bourne
   has sent the accounts all wrong,
and Everything, James says, must be gone
   into.) Such magnificent
starlight! Almost, one could see to read,
   though my glacé gloves looked quite green
—truly a wonderful display, so
   foreign, I thought, to Blue Books,
when from the chair next *ours*, utterly
   terrifying poor Bella,

a little splay-footed, *so* ugly
 dumpling of a gentleman
with a mouth from ear to ear, swaddled
 in a greatcoat *and* a shawl,
began to murmur, and would not cease,
 rattling on, ever louder,
till I guessed he must be speaking Verse!

James listened (took Bella in my *lap*
 to keep her still) and whispered
he recognized the words; we heard them
 to the last line, recited
from memory as he had it, all—
 he could not have been reading,
but abandoned himself, rather, to
 the selfish glory of it
—and by the end I caught the cadence
 too: "*No more, but fled murm'ring
and with him fled the shades of night . . .*" Then
 he broke off, sensing our eyes
were upon him. And James: "The Fourth Book,
 Sir, is it not?" He stood up,
bowed: "It is," and walked away, but stopped
 at the rail, peering up, still,
at the stars. (I doubt he had my height!)

He made a sudden gesture then, out
 over the waves and upward
to those Orbs, as if he had recalled
 something he knew and forgot
long since: "Madam," pointing to the stars,
 "Not a free Government, but
the Next Best Thing—firm and impartial
 Despotism!" On which he crossed

the foredeck and disappeared. *Tableau!*
    Was it—Macaulay? James *says*
he knows the phrase, from the new number
    of the *History*. (What it is,
to have an educated husband!
    Bella and I quite despair,
faced with such Prodigies of Learning,
    don't we?) Could it be the Great
Whig himself, and so ugly, so short? . . .

A u g u s t

. . . The mystery is solved! and in a way
    itself so mysterious!
Just today, Jane and I (and Bella)
    ventured to Cheapside to see
something of the Hippopotamus
    Murray has brought from Egypt.
One cannot but admire its prudence
    and devotion: it will *scream*
for its keeper, who must sleep next it.
    I have seen it, now, awake
and asleep—in either state it is
    certainly the ugliest
of God's works. (Bella was beside herself!)
    Like drawn unto like, perhaps?—
however the case, I was passing
    into the room with its tank,
when we were sensible of Someone—

Rather a *full* gentleman—behind us.
    "Mr Macaulay!" Jane shrieked
(she has been twice to Lady Holland's)—
    "Is that Mr Macaulay?

Never mind the hippopotamus,
  my dear!" The little fellow
 bowed quite low, and with the same gesture
   he had made on the Packet
swept in before us, but remarking
  in the sweetest of voices:
"Spare, Ladies, my modesty. I wish
  for nothing more on Earth, now
Mme. Tussaud is dead, in whose Pantheon
  I had once hoped for a place."
So much for Milton and the starry
  Pole! With a little practice
I shall "do" him, for James, to the life! . . .

S EPTEMBER

. . . I cannot free my mind, as I should,
  of those Irishry of ours,
safe at home though we are these two weeks.
  The women were so lovely,
though in rags (they never mend anything)
  and all the time they *would* scream
their meaning. It was like another
  world—nothing but ruins and
chimneys, flaming furnaces, many
  deserted but not pulled down,
and the wretched cottages around them . . .
  How I long for James to end
his Sessions and rejoin us (Bella
  is nearly an Otter now!)
while the sea is still quite warm—he could
  be *such* help, I know, dragging
that machine down the pier to shore. Bella! . . .

1864

Divisions on a Victorian Ground

A Sepoy servant, Nate, the natural son
Of my Calcutta stepfather, probably
Tended my seasickness, for I was but eight
On the long passage to England—Starboard Home.

When we called at St. Helena, he took me
A crooked way over brown hills and boulders
Till we reached a garden where we saw a man
Walking. "There he is," my black Nate said, "see him?

Buonaparte, that is he! Three pigs in a day he eats
And all the children he can lay hands on too."
Thirty years hence, to the day, I wrote the first
"Novel without a Hero." Then I was nine:

"Dear Mother, I am at Margate. This has been
Neptune Day with me. I call it so because
I go into the water and am like Neptune.
The sea was ever my friend, and shall be so.

Everyone here is very kind and *will* give
A great many cakes, a great many kisses,
But I do not let Charles kiss me. Those I take
Only from the ladies. And I learn such poems

As you once affected, the *Ode on Music,*
&c. I intend to be one of those heroes
In time" . . . In time, I have come to know Babylon,
My books made my fortune there, a kind of *Ode*

On Money. "Dress me for ten," cried the Duchess,
"Dress me for twenty!" Madam, I never make love,
I told the pretty glove-seller, I buy it
Ready-made. "Do you like London, Miss Brontë?"

And after a long pause, very gravely, "Yes
And no." Dress me for ten, dress me for twenty:
Those years upon years of world without event
Save going out to dinner, I and my wife . . .

On Sunday, sailing through the calm, shining sea
(Neptune was ever my friend, and shall be so),
Isabella, off the Isle of Wight, flung
Herself into the water (from the water-closet)

And was there twenty minutes floating before
The ship's boat even sighted her. O my God,
What a dream it is! She was found then, floating
On her back, paddling with her hands, and never

Sank at all. In the night, she made fresh attempts
At destruction, and all the first week I wore
A ribbon about my waist and fixed to hers,
The which always woke me if she moved. Marriage

Is like dipping into a pitcher of snakes
For the chance of an eel. Tennyson perhaps
Found an eel. No one else. After my seventh
Novel, it ceased to matter. I sent the boy

To Oxford with every hope he might become
A gentleman. Alas, he became only
A Roman Catholic. The girls never grew
Away from Isabella as I supposed—

She had a new kind of power, from her bed,
And seldom needed speak above a whisper.
But how they listened to her when she sighed:
"Servants talk about people, gentlefolk discuss

Things." A novelist was, she knew, beneath her.
I had not found what I wanted, nor wanted
What I found: the Grand Style for the few that meant
A small style for the many. *Punch* will show you

The rest: I was taller than Carlyle, white-haired
At forty, fond of cheroots and good claret.
I died on a visit to the Duke of Devonshire:
"Show me the Bluebeard Closet where the dead wives

Hang, and the murdered secrets. O you must have
A Bluebeard Closet! Everybody does.
Just let me sit there—I'd like that best." Today
My Jubilee Edition is "very scarce."

1876

My dearest George, you ask
for some memorials of your Uncle
         which might move the reader
      to more than a mere Impression
      of the Singular Soul he was.
I have gleaned yet again,
therefore, what to me remain more sacred
            than the bones of a Saint:
      his letters of these fifty years,
      copying out what passages
might serve for such purpose,
precious not only for the evidence
            they offer of the Man
      Within, a man whom my Brother
      perhaps too much concealed, but for
Testimony to that
entire and eager frankness which prevailed
            between us from the first.
      Choose as you will from these papers—
      to me, all that is from his hand
merits publication,
but like his answer to Froude, acknowledged
            to be the best-applied
      quotation ever made within
      five miles of the Fitzwilliam,
much may be too strictly
Classical for reproduction in print.
            Our father, you must know,
      was never a man who dealt in

38

"personal experiences"
(though it was well for him,
given the elements with which he *had*
      to deal, that Providence
    denied him in domestic life
    all sense of the ridiculous)—
hence the rueful outrage
of this scene I transcribe, to Set the Tone:
      "What I first remember,
    a baby still, was a black room
    panelled from frieze to floor with oak;
the view was east across
a park and south through an ivied window
        into a rose-garden.
    I know I stood at that window
    (the eastern one) beside Father
as a cloud of black smoke
came pouring out of the tallest chimney,
      and asked him: 'IS THAT HELL?' "
    My first recollection of him
    is that he read incessantly
from the time he was three,
lying on the rug before a great fire,
      his book flat on the floor
    and a piece of bread-and-butter
    in one hand; he wore a green coat
with red collar and cuffs,
a frill at the throat, and yellow trousers.
      The same year he went up
    to Cambridge, his letters to me
    begin, and I need intervene
no longer, though I do
recall my Brother *saying* at the time
      that if by some miracle

of vandalism all the copies of
Pilgrim's Progress & *Paradise Lost*
were destroyed off the face
of the Earth, he would vouchsafe, whenever
a revival of learning
came, to reproduce them both
from memory. That gives a sense . . .
"Political events,"
he wrote me from his College, "I can learn
regularly; but if
Lord Byron published melodies
or Scott further metrical tales,
I should never see them
or perhaps hear of them till next Christmas!
Nothing here can equal
the splendid variety of
a London Life: such, you may know,
are my sentiments, and
if ever I give the world Poetry,
it shall not be Pastoral."
One word more (I hear you, dear George,
protest my intercession) and
then your Mother is done:
Our Father, who defined a scholar as
a man who will read Plato
with his feet upon the fender,
reproved your Uncle's maiden speech
(though the House rang with cheers),
finding "ungraceful" that so young a man
should speak with *folded arms*
in the presence of royalty!
You may wonder at his bearing—
Thomas was, in those days,
a short, manly figure, marvellously

   upright, very often
  with a bad neckcloth and one hand
  in his scarlet waistcoat pocket.
I know Lady Lyndhurst
once said to him, "O Mr Macaulay,
   you are so different
  from what I expected. I thought
  you were dark, and thin, but you are
on the fair side rather,
and really, Mr Macaulay, you are fat!"
   It is true, my dear George,
  that the one exercise in which
  he can be said to have excelled
was but that of threading
crowded streets with his eyes fixed on a book!
   Reporting Milady's
  compliments he said, "on the strength
  of them, I have bought a new glass
and razor-case, and am
meditating the expediency
   of having my hair cut
  in the Burlington Arcade now.
  Yet more than a razor is needed:
I am supplied a soap
such as men of science might analyse,
   it would afford, I think,
  an excellent substitute for
  Spanish flies used in a blister.
I shaved with it, and look
in consequence as if I had that complaint
   our Mother held in horror:
  using such cosmetics often,
  I should have no choice but to beg
Queen Victoria to touch me.

Do you think she would?" In this same letter
        (often I find his most
     tender words after such teasing) :
     "News you have in all the papers.
Poor Scott is gone, and I
cannot be sorry for it. A noble mind
        in ruins is the most
     heartbreaking thing I can conceive.
     Ferdinand of Spain is gone too,
and, I fear, James Stephen—
who said once, did you know, that our Father's
        demeanor was so austere,
     if not inanimate, it was
     a riddle to which neither Gall
nor Lavater could find
the key—well, old Sir James is going fast."
        Now George, you have, of course
     all the white papers and blue-books
     from India, a mountain of meanings,
I am sure, yet for all
the significant Reform in the world,
        I must add these foothills:
     "I am glad," he wrote in answer
     to some effusion of my own,
"you have read Mme de Staël.
She was the leading woman of her age;
        Miss Edgeworth I account
     second, and Miss Austen the third . . .
     I am angry with Margaret
for grumbling as she does
at my Scriptural allusions, and still
        more angry with Nancy
     for denying me all insight
     into character. My strong point!

If she knew just how far
I see into hers, she would be ready
      to hang herself straightway!
    In this country, where *club life,*
    evenings, is a cave of despair,
in this India, we have
our share of the human miseries, baked
      annually four months,
    boiled four more, and the remaining
    four permitted to cool only
if we can 'scape being
drowned. The earth, soaked with rain, is now steaming
      like a wet horse-blanket,
    vegetation rots all round us.
    Insects and undertakers are
the only live creatures
which seem to enjoy this climate." Nowhere,
      my dear George, have I seen
    my Brother's situation so
    reported. You know that upon
his return to London
he was for many years a man acting
      so continuously
    in the face of the world that when
    his course was run, there was little
for the world to be told
about him. Your own narrative requires
      no items from me, save
    what the Duke—I wager you have
    not found *this* in Hansard—advised
on speaking in the House:
"Say what you have to say, don't quote Latin,
      and sit down." I should add
    (were the task mine, but you know best)

     this curious note: "Everybody
talks of Pagganini
and his violin these days. The man seems to be
     a miracle, and they say
    long streamy flakes of music fall
    from his strings, whence interspersed with
luminous points of sound,
they ascend the air to appear like stars.
     This eloquence is quite
    beyond me . . ." though I daresay, George,
    that for our Great Historian
it had been no such thing.
In later years, of course, your Uncle gave
     himself up entirely
    to his work, and when not abroad
    or examining battlefields,
dedicated his days
to rustic seclusion. "I used to think,"
     he wrote me from the Stour,
    "I liked London, but the truth is,
    I liked things which were in London,
and which are gone. To cease
to be a Member, only to become
     a Diner-out would be
    contemptible." Despite such ways,
    it would be difficult to give
a notion of his fame
that did him justice; perhaps this will stand:
     "An American writes
    from Arkansas, very civil
    but, by some odd mistake, directs
to me at *Abbotsford*.
Does he think all Britishers who write books
     live up there together?"

It was about this time (the first
edition of the History
was already sold out)
my Brother left his rooms in the Albany:
"My last day of lodgings.
I am sorry to leave this place,
for ever, I suppose. I may
now often use the words
for ever when I leave things. Odd that though
time is stealing from me
vigor and pleasures both, I grow
happier and happier. Milnes says,
it is shocking, it is
scandalous to enjoy life as I do.
Yet I feel I should die
best in the situation of Charles
the First, or Lewis Sixteen:
I mean, alone, beset
by enemies, and no one I cared for
near me. The parting is
the dreadful thing." And in the long
last years, your Uncle won his way
to such serenity
as only his words may convey: I send
as a proud legacy
and inspiration to your task
these last journals that Providence
has rescued from the wrack
of mortal time. You will, I know, employ
upon them all the tact
which such a trust requires of you.
May his Spirit direct your hand,
my Boy, and doing so,
delight the heart of Your loving Mother,

Louisa, Lady Trevelyan.
Herewith the diaries:
"My birthday—I am fifty. Well, I have had
a happy life indeed.
I do not know that anyone
(whom I have seen close) has had
a happier. Somewhat
I regret, but say who is better off?
Shocked to find a letter
from Dr. Holland who declares
poor Harry Hallam is dying
at Sienna. Much distressed;
I dined, however. We dine, unless the blow
comes very near the heart
Indeed . . . Met Sir Bulwer Lytton
or Lytton Bulwer, who is about
some tactic for a League
of Literary Men. I detest all such,
for I hate the notion
of gregarious authors. The less
we have to do with each other
the better. Wrote today
some of my History; not amiss, but
I am not in the stream
yet, oppressed by the weight, I fear,
of the task continuing. How odd
a thing the human mind—
mine, at least. I could write a Montaignish
queer essay upon my
morbidities—I sometimes lose
months I know not how; accusing
myself daily, yet quite
incapable of vigorous exertion.
I seem under a spell.

Then I warm, and can be working
twelve hours at a stretch! How I wrote
a year ago—and why
can I not write so now? . . . Went out, reading
Suetonius, and was
overtaken by rain and thunder.
Could not get under any tree
for fear of lightning, nor
run home for fear of bringing on tremors;
so I walked through the rain
as slowly and gravely as if
I had been a mourner in some
long funeral—my own.
Saw in the hedge the largest snake ever
I noticed in natural
liberty. O the agonies
into which the sight of a snake
creeping among the shrubs
of Barley Wood threw me, when I was six—
a serpent was to me
like a giant or a ghost: a thing
mentioned in stories, but of no
existence in England.
And the actual sight affected me
as if a goblin had
really appeared. The snake today
I followed some ways in the rain:
he seemed as much afraid
as I of his kinsman forty-four years since . . .
Walked into Herefordshire
and read while walking the last
five books of the Iliad, in tears.
Afraid to be seen crying
by parties of walkers as I came back—

crying for Achilles
cutting off his hair, for Priam
rolling on the ground—imaginary
beings merely, creatures
of an old ballad-maker who died near
three thousand years ago . . .
Evenings here a little chilly
out of doors, but the days glorious.
I rise before seven;
breakfast at nine, write a page and ramble
some five hours over rocks
and through copse-wood with Plutarch
in my hand; home for another
page; I take Fra Paolo
and sit in the garden, reading, till the sun
sinks behind Undercliff.
Then it begins to be colder,
so I carry Fra Paolo indoors,
reading on till dinner.
At table, the *Times* comes in, along with
a delicious dessert
of white peaches, abundant here.
Then a tepid stroll by starlight,
and so to bed at ten.
I am perfectly solitary, almost
as much as Robinson
before he caught Friday—have not
opened my lips that I recall
these six weeks, but to say
'Bread, if you please,' or 'Bring soda-water,'
yet I have not suffered
a moment's *ennui* . . . A visit
to Barley Wood, all greatly changed.
Shrubs not so tall as I

at eleven years old, now huge masses
        of verdure; and at points
     from which there was once a prospect,
     nothing can now be seen; the urne
of Locke has been removed.
Perhaps the place is bettered—it is not
        the place where Louisa
     and I passed our childhood. After
     dinner, returning home, I walked
late, looking at the stars
and thinking how I used to watch them so
        on board the brig *Asia*.
     Those were unhappy times, against
     these—Bombay no match for the Thames
Valley—and I find no
disposition in myself to regret
        the past, by comparison
     with the present . . ."

        Now my dear George,
     I have received the first-pulled sheets
of what you call *The Life*
of *Thomas Babington Macaulay*. George,
        it will not, *must* not do:
     Life—a life—is more than a list,
     and your Uncle, great as he was,
had that in him which made
his very greatness mean the more. You leave
        out of the reckoning
     "the thing I am shall make me live"—
     I do not hear my Brother's voice
in all your catalogue
of accomplishments, nor see him as he paused—
        it is but an instance—

before a Raphael so fine
it reconciled him (so he said)
to seeing God the Father
on canvas. Nothing of this, but Reform—
as if your Uncle lived
and died in the bleak heresy
that the world is to be ruled by
little pamphlets & long speeches.
I remember how Girtin or some other
great painter was looking
one time at a picture on which
much pains had been bestowed: "Why yes,"
he said, hesitating,
"it is very clever, well done, can't find fault,
but it wants something, wants—
why damme, it wants *that!*" throwing
his hand over his head, snapping
his fingers. You want *that,*
my boy, the vital principle I ventured
to furnish you withal.
I surrendered to your interest
(nor will I count the cost to me—
what would it signify,
the outrage of each adored remembrance,
were the world to have gained
a brighter image of the man?)
the marrow of my Brother's bones,
his inmost words, and you
return what is no more than a roll-call,
an itinerary,
a death-notice in three volumes
(bound, I warrant, in the same blue
buckram as the History!)—
Nowhere do I find my words, *his* words employed

to brighten all that waste
of Parliamentary black-letter.
I have been foolish, George dearest,
in sending what you could
not use, more foolish still in blaming you
for the ruin of my hopes,
when you have done all that was in you
to do. Biography is but
the silver-chased fittings
of a coffin, like Sir Robert Peel's smile.
My curse then, or my ban
on books, even clever ones like yours,
George: the Remains of Macaulay
remain, as they must do,
in my aspiring memory: your book
is given to the world,
while my Brother lives on in one
old woman, a tune that escapes
and an epitaph that
remains . . . as do I, your loving Mother,
Louisa Trevelyan.

1882

My dear Sir Moses, father writes, taking what time
    a rabbi may wring from his busy flock
and prompted less by his own apprehensions
    for a son than by the sense we all share
of your selfless efforts in the Great Cause whose name
    you so suitably bear—writes to tell me
(need I say how flattered I am by such concern?)
    of your kind misgivings with regard to
my engagement as conductor here at Bayreuth
    over the protests from a certain source
whose opposition persists.
                 It is true, it is
    even troublesome that the attitude
of Frau von Bülow-Wagner toward the descendants
    of Israel (among whom Rumor numbers
her husband) remains obstinate and hostile—
    she will hear of no virtue, she will close
her ears to no vice, however preposterous,
    committed by a Jew. Yet my labors
and liberties are less endangered than you fear,
    for the Meister, even in his campaign
against what he calls Judaism in Music,
    is sustained by *particular motives* . . .

Perhaps, my dear Sir Moses, I can best give you
    a suggestion of the man's true nature
and nobility—I say "perhaps" for I have
    so little time to myself, taken up
as we all are, in this place, by the unheard-of

demands of the as yet unheard *Parsifal*
which we must deal with as best we can, day by day—
    perhaps, then, I may explain (not excuse)
these special *motives*, to use a favorite word
    of Richard Wagner's, by repeating here
a story such as one I had from the father-
    in-law, old Liszt—now a Father, as well,
in religion, though I believe Rome refuses
    him the privilege of absolving sins—
who lingers, with pathetic inutility,
    about the green-room, waiting to bestow
advice which is never sought.
                        During one of these
    lapses, the listless abbé reported
(you will pardon the pun) how he bore the Meister
    off with him to Paris—this was thirty
years ago—to visit his impounded daughters.
    Cosima was but sixteen, von Bülow
unsuspected, Minna very much Frau Wagner
    still, you may imagine. "I can see them
even now," old Liszt quavered, "Cosima frightened—"
    (*I* could not see that) "—of a man who spoke
no French, a human Vesuvius, shooting out
    sheaves of flame, showers of hothouse lilies . . .
He would tease my girls, roll on the floor with the dog,
    reviling Jews the while—with him a term
of very wide meaning. I shall never forget,
    as the convent gates were locked behind us,
Wagner turned and asked if I entertained *prospects*
    for my daughter. 'None but to rescue her,'
I replied, 'from the countess her mother.' On which
    he cast down his eyes—" (who could believe that?)
"—and these were his very words: 'Late experience
    has made my own relation to the world

a negative one almost entirely. Were I
not an artist, I could become a saint—
yet this redemption is not assigned me.' And then,"
said old Liszt, "with a feverish embrace
he cried: 'Leaving that girl behind us is merely
another proof, my friend, of the great rule
by which I determine my life: *all art is but
elegy*.' " Liszt had tears in his eyes, then,
and could no more than stammer out to me: "*Ma foi,
c'était superbe*, as our poor friend Chopin
used to say."
Does it not, my dear Sir Moses, give
a worthier picture of the man than all
the Wahnfried heroics?
Judaism in Music?
My answer, having so often endured,
with Rubinstein who prepares the piano score,
Frau Wagner's excruciating remarks,
is four words: envy, terror, Jakob Meyerbeer!
Yet Providence itself appears to have
a stake in our musical history, at which
to burn the Meister's fears. For precisely
when the young King offered him the Festival House
here in Bayreuth, news came to the tavern
where Wagner was celebrating, still in a daze,
a dream of glory which was soon to come,
news that in Paris a man lay in his coffin,
bells on his wrists and ankles, and watchers
vigilant always for some sign of returning
life: Meyerbeer lay dead, the enemy Jew . . .
That, my dear Sir Moses, was Judaism in Music.

And now, as we make ready this great 'Christian Work,'
as Frau Wagner will have it called; as we

complete the rehearsals of *Parsifal* that came
    with Tristan's death into the Meister's mind;
such questions are otiose, my dear Sir Moses,
    and I feel, in response to your anxious
inquiry, that you merit an acknowledgment
    of another nature. You ask if *they*—
the Wagners, the Wagnerites—are but *using* me
    for such talents as I am known to have,
and then casting me contemptuously aside,
    once the sponge is squeezed out?
                            Dear Sir Moses,
here in Bayreuth, where bed-curtains display figures
    of Lohengrin's Swan, where *Leitmotiven*
are embroidered on shirtfronts and silk handkerchiefs,
    where the Last Supper theme, as yet unknown
to the public, is worked in gold threads on a blue
    dressing-gown, there is only one answer:
Herr Wagner is the sponge, and being squeezed by God.
    When he is empty, when this last great gift
that is in him has been . . . expressed, then it is he
    who shall be cast aside.
                            In fifty years,
my dear Sir Moses, what will it all signify
    to our children, in Germany where mine
are born and in that new Zion where you have bred
    the hope of yours? This frenzy of faction,
five decades hence, will be dispelled forever more,
    and with the Meister, with Wotan's own seed,
we shall say, or those same children say in our stead,
    enden sah ich die Welt, and mean the end
of this world to which, like Wagner's, our relations
    are no more than negative.
                            Already,
the time allowed me for such musings has elapsed,

my dear Sir Moses, and I must hasten
to Wahnfried at once for a piano rehearsal.

Convey, please, to my father all my love,
and let us share such feelings as are apposite

to a future when one need no longer
withdraw to this little Bavarian stronghold

to enjoy an art no more for Gentile
than for Jew.

Yours, dear Sir Moses,

H E R M A N N   L E V I

1889

Dear Ross, your letter arrived in the same mail
    with more drivel from Havelock Ellis
who evidently has sought from you, as well,
    the penetralia of a life he knows
to be out of the common, by admission
    if not by practice.
Can you conceive—he has also sent his quiz
    or enquiry to Swinburne. Swinburne!
Faugh! I can listen to a fellow talking
    pederasty: we understand that,
but the Lesbian!—little beast. I am
    resolved to abstain,
without appeal, from any undertaking
    in which that Pygmy has any part,
squatting in his cesspool and adding to it;
    further, I shall now endeavor
to warn you off likewise, though I have no doubt
    (as the great author
of *Justine* says of Parricide combined with
    Sodomy) these things *are* a matter
of taste. But I never in my life, besides,
    have kept a journal such as he asks
for *extracts* from: all that memory should save
    is with me best left
to the brain's own process, if there is a brain
    surviving the vexations I am
put to, and have been suffering all the while
    I tried to live in *France*. Your letter
addressed to Cannes has found me here (Hell, my dear,
    is preferable

to Cannes, Purgatory to Menton, French boys
    being far too keen in their native
perception of material advantage) . . .
    Yet what shall I say in favor of
this place in which I have, at last, *gone to ground?*
    It is a landscape
out of "Childe Roland," more like Browning's barren
    than anything you have ever seen:
bare, scored, broiled, scraped, blotched, scalped, flayed,
            flogged & ruined,
    a country calcined, grimy, powdered,
parboiled, without trees, water, grass—*with* blank
    beastly orange-groves
and senseless olive-clumps like mad cabbages
    gone indigestible. My two rooms
here in the town have seven doors in them, which
    as you open or shut them offer
a choice of sounds and sensations varying
    between the apex
of a windmill, the works of a paddle-box
    steamer and the eye of a maelstrom.
Not only Earth is brass, but also Heaven
    iron: in this accursed climate
life oozes from me, destructions by night and
    diarrhoea by day.
I live an odd fungoid life on some dead branch
    of my soul, an odoriferous
decay, eyes smarting and inflamed under blue
    spectacles and a green silk eyeshade:
the blank prose of such debility is all
    I dare write *or* read . . .
Meanwhile, my books, my blue paper, my quill pens,
    my cough, my yawnings at dawn, at dusk
my solitary pacings on the gray beach,

my languors, my martyrdoms, dear Ross,
my sickness unto death—woe to those who waste
      the best years of their
virginity in vain, *yearning* . . . O my sins
      of omission! including perhaps
some omitted sins, for these too strike me as
      mistakes, life wearing on. This morning
as I came up from the sea, Pippo rode past:
      he comes here later.
A naked boy on a naked horse, that is
      a very fine sight. I had no sense
how well the two animals suited each other.
      Yet it is only one more vision,
a vanity: I was not made to live, Ross,
      in the realm of Time.
Under this sun, at noon, when all the hot world
      which is not hugely brilliant is blue,
Priapus withers to a mere fig-tree stump,
      and I reel from one droll devotion
to another misshapen passion. Pardon
      this enthusiasm,
for that is what it is. I never narrate
      my exile without putting on strong
the Hautboys and Trumpets of my Organ, for
      it is an oppression to live here
under which I hope you may never lament,
      a deep into which
no angel can descend . . .
               This room overhangs
      the water murmuring and lapping
just beneath the window, gently at all hours;
      Pippo has left me for the last time.
Again. The point is, he has left me again:
      white flesh with green eyes,

frog-green, shining like his hair in the white air
    of afternoon, trembling in white light
reflected in the white flat sea. *La bella*
    noia! You see, the consolations
of tragedy are gone out of my life here.
    Farce is all I have;
and a few poems to write, calculated
    to make even some not over-nice
hairs stand on end, to say nothing of other
    erections equally obvious.
I tremble for the result of *your* reading,
    and cannot expect
a British public to drink out of my pond,
    even if I bring it up to their
very noses. As for an audience *here*,
    their patter has no claim to be called
articulate: it is like a man clearing
    his throat. Moreover,
there is little to be gained by pandering
    to their affected fashion (they *all*
do it so) of pronouncing their own language.
    And how I loathe their society!
Why, at one great dinner here—you know the style
    of their days: morning,
a little Mass; noon, a little dice; midnight,
    a little woman (I quite dislike
the shape of women, can scarcely bring myself
    to sketch it in a landscape study,
though it stays in the mind unconscionably)
    —I wander. At one
such party as they are forever giving
    to one another, it was the most
I could do to withhold myself from falling
    flat upon the floor and crying out:

"Behold one who is a scarecrow, I am not
     what I look to be,
tear off the clothes and flesh, find the death
     inside—you who have a God, let Him
search me, let Him scatter me to the four winds
     and scour my emptiness!" Yet I said
nothing. Why speak so? One discovers the dead
     wall in each of us,
and the great fact of my life (I know it, here)
     is that the spiritual cannot
emerge from the matter of me. Still I feel,
     within, the rebellious, unspoken
word: I will not be old. And I fall upon
     the wicked Pippo
and his kind like a man athirst. One puts them
     in good humor by offering each
a white linen suit with a red sash, telling
     them they are wanted two at a time
(always, it is safer, with these Italians,
     to arrange a choice:
one or the other is nearly sure to fail
     at the crucial moment). I confess,
myself, to a Chinese sort of love for red—
     the very names, vermillion, scarlet,
warm me, and to dress in floating crimson silk
     I half understand
being a Cardinal, a woman wholly . . .
     Enough of that life you are so good
to ask after, Ross. I leave off in order
     to belabor Ellis a bit now,
as I trust you shall do . . . You may tell people,
     if they ask you still,
I am not dead, but by no means encourage
     the notion of so much life as might

suggest human intercourse. I move as yet—
  eppur si muove!—an assiduous
mummy, from tea to dinner, making myself
    the wretched mouthpiece
of these unapprehended feelings. I have
    the contortions of the Sibyl, but
the inspiration? But the utterance?
    A mystery. My nature must be
at the root male and passionate—I want no
    affection given
which I may not return: kindness but suggests
    to the beast in me unspeakable
desires. Do not inquire too deeply of this,
    my words like my nature are obscure,
uncertain, wide of the mark that is on them.
    You know not the whole
of me, Ross, as I know not the whole of you.
    We are all and everlastingly
alone; which leads me to expect I shall make
    a good death, whereof the essence is
loneliness, and I have had sufficiency
    of practice at that.
Tell yourself, rather, the glare of contentious
    eagerness is not for me. I shall
end in the state described by the Laureate:
    'Dozing in the vale of Avalon,
and watched by weeping queens.' My dear Ross, good
                                    night.
    (Remember, Ellis
must be *stopped*. I trust you as I do myself.)

1824-1889

*The virtues which distinguish the present genera-
tion were not invented in my time.*
                    WILKIE COLLINS

The reek of a "moral hospital," something wrong
    in the nursery, the sickroom, the old men's home:
that England of your bearded friends who lay blasted
    as it might be like Ruskin and shy Carroll
by a passion for girls under twelve, like Carlyle
    by the desperate rant of wisdom that kept him
from passion at all, like Lear by the "terrible demon"
    he dared not admit—England was your Native Strain.

*Whatsoever things are snug, whatsoever things
    are influential, if there be any money: think
on these things.* You mocked them all (it was the season
    of cant and Christmas) riding around the City
in an omnibus, looking for the Actual—
    no, not looking, *glaring* was your word for Truth,
a woman in white glaring out to sea across
    the dimpled meander of the Shivering Sands.

Then later, prowling Italy with great Dickens
    and your new friends Lemon and Egg—Augustus
                    Egg!—
visiting a school for the deaf and blind, quibbling,
    while each installment kept a nation up till dawn,
over Method: *suspense* vs. *surprise*, until
    the schoolroom echoed with your shout: "Inquire of
                        them,
Charles," stabbing with your stick at the empty faces,
    "there lies your answer, there in the silent dark!"

Even amid the "festive diableries of France"
    (as Dickens winked over the Burgundy) you were
victimized by the Victorian disaster
    of your initials: all cisterns emptied behind
a door marked W.C.—here too, Household Words.
    Of all their entertainers, only you relied
not on "the white flower of a blameless life" but
    on the testimony of servants, invalids,

paupers, lunatics and foreigners. It kept you
    from being a gentleman, your *first* addiction
to an ignominy the police had known so long:
    the worst crimes of all are committed in the home,
that sanctuary out of the law's reach. *We belong,*
    you insisted—richer now than Dickens, ruder
than even Thackeray in a world of slights, and,
    after each day's Battley's Drops, your eyes bags of
                              blood—

to one great inescapable community
    of suffering. Life, you added, and kept us hanging
on every word, *was at best a hopeless disease.*
    Never marrying either mistress—not Martha
who gave you three daughters, not bourgeois Caroline
    who took up with a plumber for spite (but came
                              back)—
your only troth was plighted to Lady Laudanum,
    to whom nor gout nor Paris could make you untrue.

By the end, at bedtime, you would meet at the turn
    of the stairs, beside the bust of William Collins
R.A. on the landing, a green woman with tusks
    and a trick of biting a piece out of your neck—
her way of saying goodnight. Was it, I wonder,

surprise, by then, or suspense? It turns out you were
Actual all along, and Meredith's snide regret
    that "Wilkie was not literature" redeems you:

him we forget, who found only the real to be
    imaginable, but you remain. We need you.
"I was not only pleased and astonished," you said
    when *The Moonstone* was finished in a laudanum jag,
"but did not recognize it as my own." After
    Caroline the titular but unvisitable
mistress died, Martha Rudd, to whom you left your watch,
    your girls, and £200, tended both your graves.

1891

for Mark Strand

A storm is coming, but the clouds are still
no more than a classic custard in the west,
no closer than the sun, still august, shining
through the dishevelled branches of an oak
as if there were no darkness gathering
itself together round the scene's edges,
although the gulls come sideways, suddenly
white against the cliffs, loud in their anger.
It is the Isle of Wight, and Tennyson's Tree
("like a breaking wave?" asked Allingham,
ever poetical. "No, not in the least,"
the poet replied, peering into the leaves)
under which are sitting two old men,
the Laureate and the Signor painting him;
and being read to, both of them, by Hallam
Tennyson out of a green book, *The Golden Bough*,
published this year of the first Electrocution
(America's riposte to Gallows and Guillotine)
and the last of Parnell: it is 1891.
The Signor? Craved a name more musical
than Frith or Stubbs, and markedly more human
than Lamb or Leech or Crabbe or Hogg, unmeet
for a Grand Mannerist—"I find the laurel
also bears a thorn." Was at some pains
in the presentment of a Mortal Form
to express the lower lid, although his eyes,
with a bistre tinge around them, always looked
as if they were put in by dirty fingers:
portraits fuscous now, flat, leathery

Black Masters . . . At fifty had married a girl
of seventeen, to Save her from the Stage
(Nelly Terry—Ellen Watts—annulled) ;
at seventy, "Watts' *Hope*" a Household Word
and glory waking summer in his veins,
married again (she was twenty), the details
managed by Gracious Ladies, life and death
alike in the hands of older women. One
experience survived a thousand dinners out:
hearing some noise at midnight he remained
in darkness on the stairs, ready, stirred—
"it was the stubborn beat of wings, as if
some creature was attempting flight." Then came
a far-off voice, yet filling the air, that seemed
to cry, "Anima mia! anima mia!"—then
all was unusually still. Each time,
as even now, he told someone the story,
his blood ran brighter, like an opal warmed.
Hallam endures the venerable rudeness
(being rich in that patience the old require
of others and but rarely deserve of themselves),
reads again from the pages he cuts as he reads,
and Signor, missing half the words immersed
by the murmuring boughs, contrives to scumble in
a clump of mistletoe from the Sacred Oak,
ghostly but identifiable
over Alfred's shoulder. . . . She would come
with him, in those days, to Freshwater,
his first great inspiration, beautiful
Nelly, her hair still down, in a red straw
mushroom, the dull-red feather on it full,
lying there among the kingcups, campions
and clover just the color of that plume.
Was it not wonderful that Alfred, lately,

should see her at the Lyceum, in his *Cup*,
one face, one voice outshining all the rest
in Godwin's dresses—Nelly Godwin now,
but Ellen Terry always. He had seen her
once more himself, in splendour, through the hedge
at Little Holland House, but she had outgrown
that look of a lily with a glow-worm inside . . .
The old painter pauses, watching the setters
roll ecstatically in those campions now,
Don and Grig, snapping at each others' fleas
till the even older poet orders them off:
"What do we know of their pain, do we know
ought of the feelings of insects? They may feel
more pain than we." Hallam lays by the book,
accustomed to the signs (whose very name
had been a sign of grief he was born to bear)
and his roused father continues, righteousness
subsiding into reminiscences:
"Charles Darwin himself—decades ago
it was, a tall yellow man, sickly, dull—
could not resolve my doubts, for all his wasps
and worm-casts which will someday bury Stonehenge—
sat just where you sit, Signor, praising 'Maud'
and marvelling at my 'Miniature Edition':
I want no Species Fame, I want the warrant
of immortality." The text has shaken
Tennyson, its tale of the grove, the tree
and the grim figure with a drawn sword prowling
day and night around it, impatient
for the king to kill him, even as he killed
the king . . . "I dream of kings," he interrupts
himself, turning to Hallam: "it is true,
I suppose, that such divinity is apt
to cost them their lives . . . Priam has appeared

to me in the night." Hallam sighs. If only
someone would help him. But Signor Watts,
half deaf, stares unheeding at the cliffs,
the Coloured Rocks of Alum Bay, a smear
by this light, a stain—like something spilt.
"Priam and the rest. Not Arthur, though, no more . . .
You talk of wings, Signor: I have heard
time flowing in the middle of the night,
all things fluttering doomward, and I know
our modern fame is nothing—better have
an acre of land. I shall go down, down!
I'm up now." The Ancient Sage is blind,
the Signor cannot hear, a storm is coming.
"I feel myself to be a center, still,
and though, sometimes, of a dark morning,
I have doubts, I do believe I shall not
die."
       Who speaks? The Prospero of the Isle,
or only the Laureate? We must leave them there,
the light falters, and Mrs. Cameron—
whose photograph we have enlisted, enlarged
upon—turns away, the glass negative
held by the corners in her collodionized hands:
"Magnificent!" she whispers to herself,
"to focus them all in one picture—such an effort!"
Dark, short, sharp-eyed, we can hear her
very distinctly: "I longed to arrest the life
which came before me, and at length the longing
has been satisfied." Carlyle fumed, of course,
Browning said she made bags under his eyes,
yet there they stand, or sit, and the two old men
before us are with them: dead, immortal.
"The sun obeys your gestures," Tennyson
had told her, and her method is our own:

"Coming to a subject which, in my own eyes,
was beautiful, I stopped there, leaving all
the blur of Being on it." Away she strides
to her glass-house with the plates, both dogs
following her, and Hallam leads his father
and Signor to the Hall. The sky darkens
moment by moment, and the oak, untenanted,
surrenders to the storm at Freshwater,
August 15, 1891.

1897

An interval between the House & the Grave, deeply desired.
THE RT. HON. WILLIAM EWART GLADSTONE

That summer at Bordighera, in a fashion
somewhat agitated, he confided his dreams—
    haunted by halls and lines of people,
horrors outright, the frequent burden of which was
a weak old man gradually bruised to death by clubs.
    "What is politics in England, John,
but a long Khyber Pass, with all the misery
of a passage in," he sighed, "and no passage out?"
    We were walking the beach together,
the air was sullen, all this coast from Menton
to Santa Margharita one mild Miltonic
    hell where the welkin glistens and reeks,
every surface swelters until Earth's face cracks,
and only the Sea is whole, running high along
    the sand, huge green masses of water
shattering to mere foam at our feet. In this heat
who would expect such a sea? Mr. G delights
    in it, has a passion for its sound,
would like to have it in his ears all day, all night:
"It is the truth of Dante's *Banquet*, my boy, where
    the noble soul is said to be like
a good mariner, for he, when he draws near port,
lowers his sails and enters softly, with gentle
    steerage." It is his way of speaking
I can catch, though I am separated from him
in the order of ideas by an interval
    that must be called a gulf. Forgive me
if I go too far—I am simply a funnel,

my local memory has always been vivid,
  I seem never to have forgotten
a circumstance, a scene, a single syllable,
for all my personal rank as a vanishing
    quantity—why else should Mr. G
have kept me with him past his years of employment,
years of Parliamentary meddle and muddle?
  "In the long run, John, we are all dead;
memoirs are as hateful to me as monuments,
but a memory like yours is another thing."
  Striding down the beach desecrated
by gold-necked bottles, lobster claws, bits of veal pie,
he would ask me to prod him into reckoning
    of what has been his life. Eighty-eight
years have deterred none of his senses, save perhaps
that of . . . reality: the man is a great white rock
    with a little moss on it, just so,
and the green sea-water beneath. One word of mine
suffices to release, like some bottled *djinni*,
    that affluent language he bestows
so effortlessly. Once, indeed, he admitted
speculating why the room seemed to fall silent—
    "only to discover I had stopped
talking. It was a genuine discovery."
The word, this time, was some trifling *bon mot* of mine
    on the Heir Apparent's appearance.
That was enough: "Three decades of Her Majesty's
crisp, incessant orders, John, have convinced me quite
    of the unfailing, the shall I say
hereditary antipathy of our sovereigns
to their heirs apparent. The single time I dined
    with the Prince and his mother, a swan—
very white and tender, stuffed with truffles as well—
was the best company at table, and the **Queen's**

sole remark to her son (and myself)
was that dogs behaved better to the furniture
than in the past . . . the one improvement quite certain
    in modern times. Ah, my boy," he groaned,
"we are well away from Balmorality here,
the terrible Tartanitis which overtook
    the Throne in my time, hard upon
the Morte d'Albert. Remarkable statesman, mind you,
but the stock was weak. You recall the cousin, Ludwig
    of Bavaria? Talked with his eyes
tight shut. Drowned himself in the ornamental lake
with his doctor. No stamina in the family.
    Though the Queen is of the family,
and endures . . . Her words to me, when I took my leave—
simple perfection of perfect simplicity:
    'Often, Mr. Gladstone, I believe,
after a period of strenuous reform,
a moment comes, quite suddenly, when the British
    people tires of being, ah, *improved*.'
Thank God, John, I am quit of all such encounters."
And then, as we proceeded to the pier from which
    a superb view might be had, waves
hurling themselves over each other to the rocks,
he took from an inner pocket, with a sharp glance
    into my eyes, a green morocco
notebook quite glossy with wear. "I was but eighteen,
John, when I entered these words. Judge, if I have
    kept faith with those emotions of mine."
The diary was in his backhand, tiny script,
unchanged subsequently. "On board the *Queen of Scotland*.
    Rose to breakfast, but uneasily.
Attempted reading, first book of Herodotus,
not too unwell to reflect. Returned to bed, then
    translated a few lines of Dante.

Also, Beauties of Shakespeare. By evening, high wind
blowing. Quite ill, though still in bed. Yet could not help
    admiring the white crests of the waves,
even as I stood at the cabin's low casement."
He took it from me with a gesture to the sea,
    and we walked on, Mr. G gloating
in the huge force, the swell and beat of the rollers
on the shore, like a titanic pulse. As they ran,
    bounding toward us with bright persuasions
of grace and power, he wondered if we had not more
and better words for the sea than the French language:
    "*flot, vague, onde, lame,* as against
breaker, billow, comber, bore, eagre, roller, swell
and surge." He quite shouted the words into the tide.
    I have never seen him so happy.

1907

A Proposal from Paris

Herr Privatdozent, it is not my way
                    to intervene
          in matters of this nature:
our livelihood
is, after all, our very life—I know.
                    Yet so truly
          inviting is the venture
I would have you
embark upon that I must run the risk . . .
                    As a German
          musician, hear my offer,
my *overture*,
which it must indeed be called. Yes, but first
                    let me tell you
          how it has all come about.
I am writing
from our bedroom—*Jugendstyl*, pink satin—
                    overlooking
          Place Vendôme, where all the new
leaves cannot yet
keep the Column out there from suggesting
                    what a column,
          my wife reminds me, always
suggests. Aside
from such obscenities, we are left quite
                    undisturbed here,
          and for a French impresario
I must admit
Astruc has been generous, though perhaps
                    imagining

us both more susceptible
to coronets
than to *Kröner,* if you take my meaning.
            After last night's
performance of *Salome*
(the last of five
by which I introduced my Prinzessin
                to her public
    here), I was to have the bulk
of my fee, but
found instead the *loge d'artistes* filled with
            loud duchesses.
    There was the usual furor,
and it may be
that in the confusion I let myself
                become somewhat
        overwrought. In any case,
when the trollope
who is Astruc's mistress and doubles for
            Emmy Destinn
    during the Dance requested
a solo bow,
I reminded her (and the company)
            that dancing was,
        really, an inferior art,
requiring no
special notice from a public applauding
            Frau Destinn and—
        yes, I said as much—myself.
"If anything,"
the harlot answered, "is inferior"
                —these are her words—
    "it is the masquerading
of a self-styled

genius who comes on stage every night,
             making his bows
     to a house that does not ask
him to appear."
At which my Pauline (you know how forthright
             she is at times)
     went up and administered
two ringing slaps
that brought the blood to Trouhanova's cheeks.
             "We have not yet
     sunk so low," she smiled, taking
my arm, "that we
need be insulted by the Seraglio."
             We left the house,
     and need I say, the francs were
waiting for us
by the time we reached the Ritz. —You will think
             I am forgetting,
     dear friend, but I bear in mind,
through all the din
and distractions of Paris, my purpose,
             which is to win
     you over to an idea,
or an *ideal*,
so tempting that were it not for the last
             of *Elektra*—
     her dance of triumph and death—
I am not sure
I should even afford you this Great Chance.
             The next evening,
     you see, after *my* series,
Romain Rolland
(a pacifist!) and some handsome jockey
             of a fellow

named Ravel invited me
to the so-called
masterpiece of the new French school, revived
at the Comique:
Pelléas et Mélisande.
Nikisch, also,
was in the house, and how I look forward
to *his* account
of the deplorable fraud . . .
After three scenes
I leaned over, pulled Ravel's sleeve; the man
(to call him that)
is a kind of Narcissist
who reduces
all his needs to a few physical charms,
and even there
in the dim *baignoire* I think
I could make out
that he was rouged and powdered, and I *know*
he was perfumed.
Overcoming my distaste,
I questioned him:
"Is it like this throughout?" "Yes." "Nothing more?"
"Nothing." (proudly!)
"Then," I permitted myself
to inform him,
"There's nothing in it—no development,
no melody,
no consecutive phrases . . ."
"There *are* phrases,"
he had the effrontery to tell me,
"only hidden."
At this, my French quite failed me:
"First and foremost,

I am a musician," I replied, "and
   I hear nothing.
  Of course it is very . . . (here
I had to fall
back on our own) . . . *gekunstet,* but never
    spontaneous,
  there is no . . . no *Schwung* in it
(I defy you,
Herr Privatdozent, to find a French word
    proper for *Schwung*)
  —one might as well be hearing
only the words,
the prose of Maeterlinck." —And that, dear friend,
   is why I write . . .
  Knowing your gifts as I do,
I conjure you
to take this very subject, *Pelléas*
   und Mélisande:
  precisely in those places
where Debussy's
mood-murmurs misfire—the lovers' farewell,
    then the murder—
  there you will write one Big Scene
after the next.
I promise you there's music in the piece
   after your own
  passion for nobility,
for heroic
renunciation—the thing lies ready
   to your hand, just
  as it jostles mine, although
von Hofmannsthal
is waiting, and I dare not . . . You may guess,
   the houselights up,

how Ravel melted away
like a pale wisp
of patchouli, and Rolland took me round
to Debussy.
What was it I expected?
One of Khnopff's heads,
or a Klimt: some Celt with periwinkles
of the abyss
in his eyes—here was a gnome
in a sack suit,
carved out of one thick black radish. They say
his wife's money
is what he lives on—like Wagner,
in blue velvet.
And how *could* this Dekadent tell the tale—
I remind you,
only to torment myself:
the lovers meet,
every shadow, every sound a terror
when they embrace,
and that is when she sees him:
"Golaud, Golaud—
where our shadows end!" but will not escape.
Love is the death
they share—does it remind you?
And Pelléas
takes her lips again, again, the stars fall . . .
and Golaud falls
upon the lovers, cuts down
Pelléas, then
crashes through the forest pursuing her . . .
Let it be yours,
my dear Herr Privatdozent,
since it may not

be mine—but never Monsieur Debussy's,
> promise me that!
>   Pauline joins me in sending,
now as always,
our devoted regards. Yours,
>   RICHARD STRAUSS

1915

A Pre-Raphaelite Ending, London

for Sanford Friedman

Save it all; you do not know
the value things will come to have until
the world grows dim around you, and your things
—however doubtful in the changing light,
> things are what you have
> left. And all you have.
Once the Zeppelins are gone
—and I shall be gone too, then, surely gone
out of this chair, this bed, this *furniture*,
there will be time enough to throw away
> whatever is left.
> Keep the papers here
in these boxes where I have
kept them so long to myself—for myself,
till the Zeppelins. I am not certain
(how could I be, kept here out of harm's way)
> what Zeppelins *are*.
> You would not expect
the daughter of an Oxford
livery-stable keeper to know it . . .
Your father was not fond of animals.
He said once he might get to like a horse,
> if he had the time.
> Take care with the ones
on top, they are photographs.
Read out what is scrawled there: "Dearest Janey,
Dodgson will be here tomorrow at noon,
do come as early as you can manage."
> They have no backing

and break like dead leaves.
Often Gabriel painted
from these when he could not see me. He said
Mr. Dodgson knew what to leave out. Give
that one to me. No, it does not matter.
                    I want to hear you
                    say the words aloud:
    "Absence can never make me
so far from you again as your presence did
for years. Yet no one seems alive now—
the places empty of you are empty
                    of all life." Of course
                    William knew of it,
    but trusted. He had a deep
understanding of one side of life, and
invented the other. Remember how
he loved to list the things he owned,
                    grade and tabulate . . .
                    Why, he could not sit
    in this room without an arm
about my waist—when others were by. Then
one time he burst out in a rage: "Is it
nothing but make-believe, am I no more
                    than Louis XVI
                    tinkering with locks?"
    You know what his rages were—
I saw him drive his head against that wall,
making a dent in the plaster. "With locks,"
he said, "tinkering with locks, and too late . . ."
                    With locks, did he say,
                    or clocks? Clocks, I think.
    How can a woman resolve
her marriage, save by lies? I have not learned
from others. I speak of my own life. She

stays at home, the man goes forth. A husband's
                    absence, a daughter's
                    anger, a lover's
        suspicion—that is her lot.
What survives is the resistance we bring
to life, the courage of our features, not
the strain life brings to us. Each doctor says
                    a different thing
                    when I awaken
        gasping in the night. How well
one has to be, to be ill! *Tragic health,*
Mr. Ruskin called it. That is his hand,
I recognize the stroke. He gave me this
                    during a long walk
                    after Gabriel
        was cold in his grave, at last.
No one may see them till after my death,
and you must wait for that. William waited,
but I have not died. He came to Kelmscott
                    —the meadows flooded
                    that year, and the noise
        of water filled the air. "Jane,
I wegwet," he said—he could not pronounce
his r's, odd in a man named Ruskin. Then
a tortoise-shell butterfly settled on
                    my shoulder, but he
                    refused to notice.
        "I cannot admire any
lower in the scale than a fish," he said,
"I have the best disposition toward slugs
and gnats, but why they exist I do not
                    understand." He stopped,
                    though, to pick some cress
        growing by the path—and what

he regretted was that he could not bear
to destroy these drawings he would give me
on the condition that I never look
                    at them in my life.
                    They must be naked
        drawings of me, beautiful
indeed if Mr. Ruskin could not burn
what he bought to keep the world and William
from seeing. There are his words on the seal:
                    "I should as soon try
                    finding fault with him
            as with a nightshade-blossom
or a thundercloud. Of him and of these
all I can say is that God made him, and
they are greatly made: To me they may be
                    dreadful or deadly.
                    There is certainly
            something wrong with him—awful
in proportion to the power it affects
and renders at present useless. So it was
with Turner, so with Byron." With this came
                    a great quantity
                    of ivory-dust
        to be made into a jelly,
which it seems is an excellent physic
for invalids. Not even William failed
to guess the shame beneath the show—
                    he had the habit,
                    months and years after,
        of taking up the packet
and regarding its black seal with the eye
of an enemy. I was like Mariana
in the moated grange, listening too often
                    to the mouse shrieking

in the wainscot. "I
can't paint you but I love you—"
he said that when I sat to them, at Oxford.
He first saw me there, and his destiny
was defined . . . Gabriel called him a name:
Tops, the poetic
upholstery-man.
Their mothers all outlived them—
Gabriel, William, *and* Mr. Ruskin.
It was an abyss then, an imbroglio
then and after. The reciprocal
life of "well persons"
grew impossible.
Moments come when the pattern
is laid before us, plain. And then we know
the limitations, accidentally
repeated, are the stuff of life. They will
return again, for
they are just . . . ourselves.
Then we know that this and none
other will be our life. And so begins
a long decay—we die from day to dream,
and common speech we answer with a scream.
Put those things aside.
Here are the letters
from Iceland, times were mended
for us both, by then. William was away
from the loud group of yellowing rowdies
who called themselves "communists"—and from me.
And he wrote, always,
lovely letters—if
you did not have to hear him
say the words, as if he were breaking off
bones, throwing them aside—it was, through him,

an ancient voice speaking, or a voice from
    a previous life
     jerking the words out
 of a body which it had
nothing to do with. Take one from the lot,
they are all the same, though like no one else:
freeing ourselves we forge our own chains.
     "I lie often out
     on the cliffs, lazy
  themselves, all grown with gold broom,
not athletic as at Dover, not gaunt
as at Shields, and through the mist of summer
sea and sky are one, while just underfoot
     the boats, together,
     stand immovable—
 as if their shadows clogged them.
So one may lie and symbolize until
one falls asleep, and that be a symbol
as well." Take the last one. I remember
     the last words the best.
     "As for living, dear,
  people like those you speak of
don't know what life means or death either, save
for one or two moments when something breaks
the crust, and they act for the time as if
     they were sensitive."
     William's mind was set
 on things more significant
than human lives, individual lives . . .
During the last illness, Dolmetsch came here
to play Byrd to him on the virginals.
     He broke into tears
     —of joy, only joy,
 at the opening phrases

of a pavane. Then he saw white bodies
moving, crowned and bound with gold. That faded.
I went for the post, and when I returned
                  he stifled the blood
                  streaming from his mouth
  and held fast to my gown, one
of his designs I had worn all those days.
"The clothes are well enough," were his last words,
"but where has the body gone?" Is there more
                  besides, in the box?
                  I thought not. Will you
    do as I say, save it all—
the rest of the things are mere images,
not medieval—only middle-aged:
lifelike but lifeless, wonderful but dead.
                  These are mine. Save them.
                  I have nothing save them.